Curious George®
The Donut Delivery

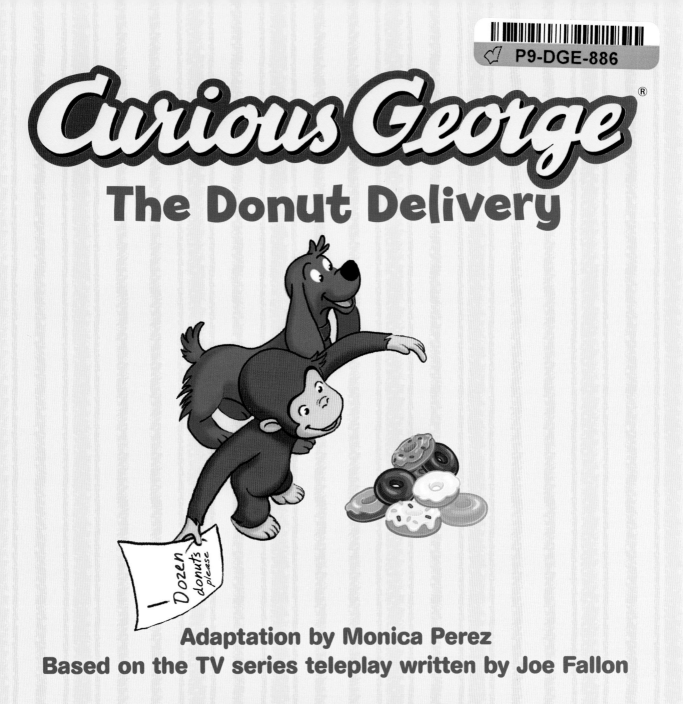

I Dozen donuts please

Adaptation by Monica Perez
Based on the TV series teleplay written by Joe Fallon

Houghton Mifflin Company, Boston

For information about permission to reproduce selections from this book, write to trade.permissions@hmhco.com or to Permissions, Houghton Mifflin Harcourt Publishing Company, 3 Park Avenue, 19th Floor, New York, New York 10016.

Library of Congress Cataloging-in-Publication Data

Perez, Monica.
Curious George: The donut delivery / adapted by Monica Perez ; based on the TV series teleplay written by Joe Fallon.
p. cm.
ISBN-13: 978-0-618-73757-4 (pbk. : alk. paper)
ISBN-10: 0-618-73757-X (pbk. : alk. paper)
I. Fallon, Joe. II. Title.
PZ7.P42583Cus 2006
2005038070

Design by Joyce White
www.hmhco.com

Printed in China
SCP 17 16 15 14 13 12 11
4500818785

George is always a good monkey—when he's asleep. But no monkey wants to sleep through Saturday. This was a Saturday that cried out for something special . . .

"Donuts!" the man with the yellow hat announced.
That was special. Next to bananas, donuts were George's favorite food.
"How about eggs with those donuts?" the man asked George. "Please count
how many we have and write it down."

But when George looked for the eggs, he found there were none left to count.
"There are no eggs?" the man asked. "Why didn't you write zero?"
George didn't know how.

The man with the yellow hat sat George down with some paper and a pad.
"See, George," the man said, "zero ALONE means no eggs. None.
But zero after other numbers makes them mean a lot more.

If we put a zero after one, that's ten. Write another zero, and that's a hundred."
George stared hungrily at the zeros. They reminded him of donuts!

**Luckily for George and his empty stomach, they headed out to buy the groceries.
The man stopped in front of a market. He said, "I'll go in here and buy eggs
while you get the donuts. Okay?"**

George nodded as the man wrote down his order. The note said, "1 dozen donuts, please."

As George headed to the donut shop, Charkie, a friendly little dog from the neighborhood, joined him. She wanted to play, but George was too busy to stop. So she followed him into the shop.

George noticed that his order only had a little "1" on it. That did not seem like a lot for a monkey who was really hungry. George saw a pencil on the counter. He grabbed it and drew a zero after the "1." Now the note read, "10 dozen donuts."

Then George wrote down another zero before Mrs. D came to take his order.

"George, Charkie, good to see you. Is that an order for your friend with the yellow hat?"

George handed over the paper.

"One hundred dozen donuts!" she exclaimed. "That's our biggest order ever!"

Mrs. D hurried away to tell her husband in the kitchen.

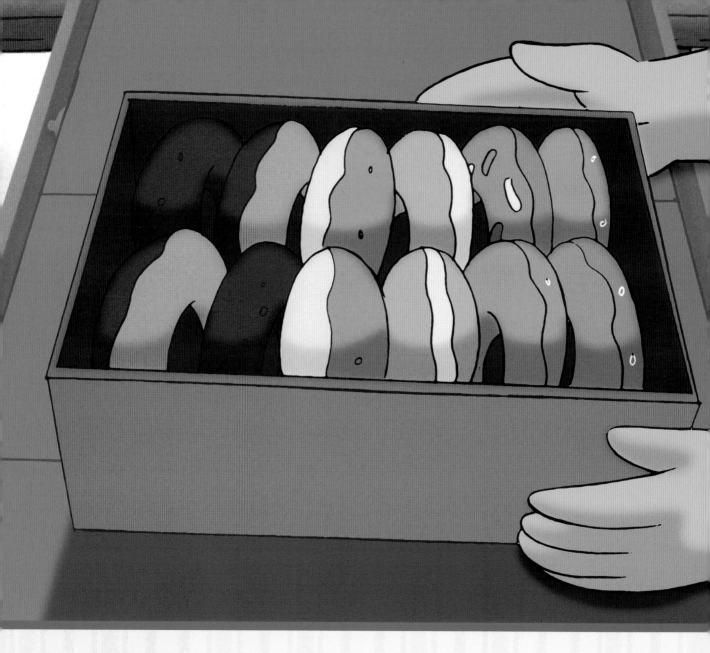

Soon Mrs. D started piling box after box on the counter. George grew worried. He hadn't realized what his zeros would do.

". . . Ninety-nine, one hundred. You can't possibly carry them all, George," Mrs. D said. "Lucky for you we have a delivery service!"

Mrs. D bustled off to get some help, but George did not wait around. He grabbed one dozen donuts and ran away with Charkie.

George was not quick enough. Mrs. D's entire family was soon right behind him with their towering boxes of donuts.

"He must be running late! We took too long to make the donuts!" Mrs. D cried as she rushed after George.

When George reached his apartment, he jumped from balcony to balcony, trying to get home as quickly as possible.

At first George thought he was safe from the donut delivery. He sat down to catch his breath after running all the way home. But it wasn't long before the doorman showed the D family right up to his apartment!

Soon a hundred boxes of donuts crowded the room. George looked around. He had to do something before his friend came home. Suddenly, he had an idea.

When the man with the yellow hat walked in carrying his groceries, he saw only one box of donuts on the table. "Those smell so good," the man said. "I'm sorry I didn't ask you to buy more than one dozen."
Was George able to hide all those donuts?
Not for long. George explained to the man that he had added some zeros to the order.
"Well, at least you learned something," the man said. "But what are we going to do with all these donuts?"

They came up with a good solution. George got one dozen donuts like he was supposed to . . . and some hard-working firefighters got the rest.
"How many left, George?" the man asked at the end of the day. George ate the last donut from a box and held up his fingers in an "o" shape. Zero!

DONUT PLACE VALUE

Adding a zero to a number really means you are multiplying or counting by ten. Count the number of donuts to find the answer to the math problem. Then have fun coloring them in!

1 x 10 = 1____

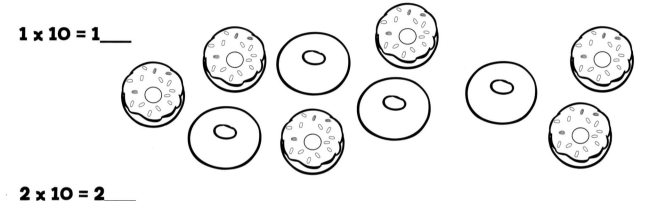

2 x 10 = 2____

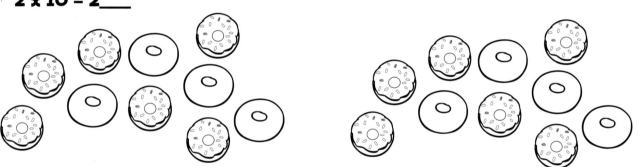

3 x 10 = 3____

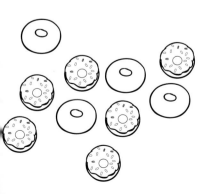 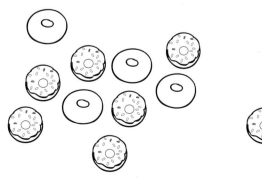 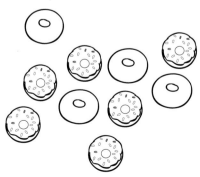

THE POWER OF TEN

Ask your parent to exchange a one-dollar bill at the bank for two rolls of pennies. Each roll should contain fifty pennies. Using all the coins, make several piles of ten pennies each. **How many piles do you end up with?** _____

Now take your answer and put it into the problem below to find out how many pennies you have in all.
(You can count all the pennies to check if you solved the problem correctly.)

10 pennies in each pile x _____ piles = _____ pennies total

See how useful zero can be? It can turn one penny, or one cent, into ten pennies, or ten cents. It can turn ten pennies, or ten cents, into one hundred pennies, or one dollar.

Useful facts to remember:
1 x 10 = 10
10 x 10 = 100
1 penny = 1 cent
10 pennies = 10 cents
100 pennies = 1 dollar

 Time to put your pennies into your piggybank!